D1607339

WHAT ARE DIFFERENT TYPES OF COMMUNITIES?

JOSIE KEOGH

Britannica®
Educational Publishing

IN ASSOCIATION WITH

ROSEN
EDUCATIONAL SERVICES

Published in 2018 by Britannica Educational Publishing (a trademark of Encyclopædia Britannica, Inc.) in association with The Rosen Publishing Group, Inc.
29 East 21st Street, New York, NY 10010

Distributed exclusively by Rosen Publishing.
To see additional Britannica Educational Publishing titles, go to rosenpublishing.com.

First Edition

Britannica Educational Publishing
J.E. Luebering: Executive Director, Core Editorial
Mary Rose McCudden: Editor, Britannica Student Encyclopedia

Rosen Publishing
Bernadette Davis: Editor
Nelson Sá: Art Director
Matt Cauli: Designer
Ellina Litmanovich: Book Layout
Cindy Reiman: Photography Manager
Sherri Jackson: Photo Researcher

Library of Congress Cataloging-in-Publication Data

Names: Keogh, Josie, author.
Title: What are different types of communities? / Josie Keogh.
Description: First edition. | New York, NY : Britannica Educational Publishing, 2018. | Series: Let's find out! Communities | Includes bibliographical references and index.
Identifiers: LCCN 2016058548| ISBN 9781680487312 (library bound : alk. paper) | ISBN 9781680487299 (pbk. : alk. paper) | ISBN 9781680487305 (6-pack : alk. paper)
Subjects: LCSH: Communities — Juvenile literature.
Classification: LCC HM756 .K46 2018 | DDC 307 — dc23
LC record available at https://lccn.loc.gov/2016058548

Manufactured in the United States of America

Photo credits: Cover, p. 1, interior pages (background) RudyBalasko/iStock/Thinkstock; p. 4 Sean Xu/Shutterstock.com; p. 5 Buyenlarge/Archive Photos/Getty Images; p. 6 jiratto/Shutterstock.com; p. 7 Andrey Bayda/Shutterstock.com; p. 8 katatonia82/Shutterstock.com; p. 9 The Washington Post/Getty Images; p. 10 Cameron Davidson/Photographer's Choice/Getty Images; p. 11 jiawangkun/Shutterstock.com; p. 12 © iStockphoto.com/Dean Mitchell; p. 13 Sean Pavone /Shutterstock.com; p. 14 chiakto/Shutterstock.com; p. 15 Federico Rostagno/Shutterstock.com; p. 16 Barry Winiker /Photolibrary/Getty Images; p. 17 Boston Globe/Getty Images; p. 18 © iStockphoto.com/VisualCommunications; p. 19 Richard Nowitz/National Geographic/Getty Images; p. 20 Michael Rosebrock/Shutterstock.com; p. 21 Prisma /Superstock; p. 22 Emi Cristea/Shutterstock.com; p. 23 National Geographic Creative/Bridgeman Images; p. 24 Everett Historical/Shutterstock.com; p. 25 Museum of Science and Industry, Chicago/Archive Photos/Getty Images; p. 26 rarrarorro/Shutterstock.com; p. 27 © iStockphoto.com/SolStock; p. 28 © iStockphoto.com/cyano66; p. 29 Blend Images/Alamy Stock Photo.

CONTENTS

TYPES OF
COMMUNITIES

In science, the word "community" refers to living things that live together and rely on one another for survival. Humans can be a part of many different kinds of communities. Each community affects how its members live their daily lives. For instance, if you live

Rural communities, like this one in Colorado, sometimes have beautiful scenery.

in a city, or urban community, you could see hundreds of people every day. But if you live in a rural community, you may see a dozen people every day.

A city is a concentrated center of population that includes a variety of workplaces, schools, and residential buildings. Built-up areas called suburbs lie outside the boundaries of most big cities. Rural communities are in the countryside. They have a lower population than cities and suburbs do.

Big cities like this one are crowded with many different types of buildings.

THINK ABOUT IT

Do you have friends or family members who live in a different type of community than you do?

CITIES

A city is a place where people live closely together. New York City is the largest city in the United States. Other big American cities are Los Angeles, Chicago, and Houston. Toronto is the biggest city in Canada. Tokyo, Japan, has more people than any other metropolitan area in the world.

A city's central business district, or downtown, usually has its tallest office buildings and biggest stores. The downtown area is often the oldest part of the city. A city usually has one or more areas with

The city of Tokyo is part of the huge Tokyo metropolitan area.

6

New York City has many famous sites. Times Square is famous for its theaters and bright lights.

factories and warehouses (storage buildings) outside of downtown. Most of the city's homes lie still farther from downtown.

Cities usually have a variety of places for entertainment and relaxation. These include museums, concert halls, theaters, parks, and sports arenas.

City life has many benefits. Cities bring together a great variety of people from different backgrounds. They attract people looking for work, education, and other ways to improve their lives. They bring together many talented people. Cities are therefore often centers of invention, artistic creation, acceptance, and social change.

City life can also be hard. Not everyone shares equally in the benefits of the city. Some people live

Cities are home to a wide mix of people with different backgrounds and interests.

in rundown, overcrowded housing. Others have no homes at all. They sometimes live on the streets. Crowded living conditions in cities sometimes also lead to crime, heavy traffic, and pollution.

This family is living in a hotel that houses the homeless in Washington, DC.

Many people in cities work to try to solve these problems. Local governments and private groups provide funds to operate homeless shelters and soup kitchens. Community groups run programs to combat violence and poverty.

THINK ABOUT IT

Do you think that the benefits of living in a city outweigh the problems? Why or why not?

Suburbs

Suburbs surround cities and are part of a city's metropolitan area. Suburbs may be towns, villages, or small cities. They have their own local governments and services such as police and fire protection. People who live in the suburbs often commute, or travel for work, to the city. This is because cities supply many of the jobs for people who live in the suburbs.

There are many differences between life in a city and life in a suburb. People often

Houses in the suburbs often have front yards *and* backyards.

Some people who live in the suburbs travel on trains to reach their jobs in cities.

move from the city to the suburbs as they get older and have children because they want more space. The suburbs usually offer larger homes with grassy yards and better-funded public schools. However, suburbs tend to be more expensive and often residents must have a car to get around.

COMPARE AND CONTRAST

How are cities and suburbs alike? How are they different?

Rural Areas

Rural areas are also known as the country. They are large areas of land with few houses or businesses. They often do not have as many services as cities and suburbs. People may have to travel long distances to the nearest grocery store, doctor, or school.

There are many reasons people like living in rural communities. Some enjoy the peace and quiet. Others appreciate being close to nature and outdoor

Many rural communities have good fishing spots.

12

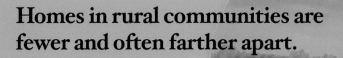

Homes in rural communities are fewer and often farther apart.

activities, such as hunting, fishing, and hiking. Many rural residents appreciate the slower pace of life and the cheaper cost of living. While rural communities are small, they are usually close-knit. People depend on and help out their neighbors. Today, people in rural areas can stay connected to people beyond their community as well through access to the internet and satellite television.

THINK ABOUT IT

How was life in rural areas different before people in those areas had access to the internet?

Many people in rural communities have jobs that involve natural resources. Farmers grow food and raise animals. Some people work in logging, cutting down trees. The wood from the trees is used to make lumber for building things or turned into pulp that is used to make paper. Other people extract fossil fuels, such as oil, coal, and natural gas. Some rural areas are major sources of mineral resources, such as copper and iron ore.

These job options mean that rural life can be hard. Advances in agriculture have reduced the need for human workers on farms

These men are working in a silver mine. Mines can be dangerous places to work.

Almost all of the food that people eat is grown on farms that are in rural areas.

and ranches. The coal mining and logging industries are struggling, too. People have moved away from some rural areas because of that. Other people like to live in rural areas and travel into cities to work or connect to offices in cities through the internet.

LOCAL GOVERNMENTS

Municipal governments organize and run local communities. A municipality is a city, town, or village that is self-governing. In some cases a county can be a municipality. Counties are called boroughs in Alaska and parishes in Louisiana.

The structure of municipal governments varies from country to country. In the United States, it also varies from state to state. A municipal government

Municipal governments often meet in a town hall, city hall, or municipal building.

16

Citizens can speak at some city council meetings.

for a town may include a group of elected lawmakers called a town council. One for a city would be called a city council. Many municipalities elect a leader called a mayor. In some towns the mayor has a lot of power, while in others the mayor is just the chairperson of the town council. In some cities a city manager—the city council usually picks this person—is in charge of most governmental matters.

THINK ABOUT IT

What kind of municipal government does your community have?

Municipal governments provide many services. These include police and fire protection, hospitals, and schools. Many municipalities collect residents' garbage, clear snow from roads, and build and maintain streets, sidewalks, parks, and playgrounds.

THINK ABOUT IT

Rural communities have smaller, more spread-out populations. These communities tend to provide fewer services than suburban and urban ones. Why do you think this is?

Different municipalities provide different services. The larger the municipality, the more services it is called upon to provide. Large cities have their own libraries, museums, zoos, historical societies, and other cultural attractions. To attract and keep businesses, they often

Some towns and cities hire snow plows in the winter.

18

This sign directs visitors to some of the tourist attractions in Washington, DC.

build sports arenas and convention centers.

Municipalities pay for services by charging fees and collecting taxes from the people who live there. Wealthy communities are able to provide more services than poorer ones. For example, well-off suburban towns may be able to afford new books and computers for schools, while struggling cities or rural areas make do with old computers and used books.

TRANSPORTATION

Transportation is how people get to where they need to go. People depend on various forms of transportation to get to school and work. On top of these almost-daily trips, people also need to get to stores to buy food, clothes, and other goods. When they are sick or hurt, people need to get to a hospital or doctor.

In some cities people can use streetcars to get around.

Cities commonly have a public transportation system to help people get around without cars. Public transportation includes buses, trains, subways, and streetcars. Subways are trains that run underground. Streetcars run along tracks in a street. In rural areas and suburbs, most people depend on their own cars and trucks to get around. However, rural and suburban students often travel to and from school in school buses.

Almost all school buses in the United States are an easy-to-spot bright yellow.

COMPARE AND CONTRAST

How are buses like cars and trucks? In what ways are they similar to trains and subways?

CHANGES OVER TIME

Communities change over time. The first settlers in different areas around the world had to find safe places to live that would provide them with the resources they needed, such as water, building materials, and good land for farming. Over time, roads and footpaths developed between villages as people traded with one another. Some villages grew into towns or cities, while others disappeared completely.

About 5,500 years ago people in Mesopotamia

The city of Rome, in Italy, is thousands of years old.

(now Iraq) started the first cities. Some cities in ancient times were independent of any country. They were called city-states. City-states ruled themselves and their surrounding area. Athens and Sparta were major city-states of ancient Greece. From the 1000s to the 1400s, Florence, Venice, and other city-states were important in what is now Italy. Later, city-states lost their independence. Today almost all cities belong to a particular country.

COMPARE AND CONTRAST

How were city-states like modern cities? How were they different?

The Industrial Revolution, which started in the late 1700s, contributed to the growth of cities. New machines invented during this period made manufacturing an important business. Many people from the countryside moved into cities. They looked for work in newly built factories.

In the late 1800s architects invented new building methods that changed the way cities looked. Tall buildings called skyscrapers appeared in many cities. During the 1900s cities continued to change. They grew rapidly in population. They also spread outward. Many people moved to the suburbs. Some highly populated areas became known as megalopolises. Megalopolises

This drawing shows one of the factories set up during the Industrial Revolution.

The Home Insurance
Building, in Chicago,
was an early skyscraper.

often include several cities and many suburbs.

Today, urban and suburban areas are growing more quickly than rural ones. This is likely because more jobs are available in urban and suburban communities. While some jobs are in manufacturing, more are in industries that serve the public, such as banking, health care, and communications.

So Many Communities

The town or city that you live in is not the only community to which you belong. After all, any group of people with a common interest or shared experience is a community. The people who are students or teachers at a particular school make up a school community. They all want to make their school a safe, welcoming place to learn.

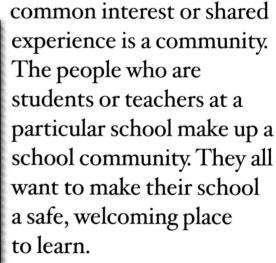

Chinatown is the center of San Francisco's Chinese American community.

People from the same background make up a community too. For example, a person might be a member of the African American community, the Italian-American community, or the Puerto Rican community.

Religion also creates communities. Examples include the Jewish, Muslim, and Hindu communities. The people who go to a particular house of worship make up a religious community, too. Communities of monks or nuns living together are yet another kind of religious community.

This is a community in a school building.

THINK ABOUT IT

How many communities do you consider yourself to be part of?

People form all sorts of communities. Members of the army, navy, and air force are part of the military community. Musicians are members of the general music community. They also belong to a community of a specific genre (or type) of music such as the hip-hop community or the country music community. People don't even need to meet in person to be part of a community. People who talk to each other online make up online communities.

The members of an orchestra make up a community.

During a food drive, people collect food for those in need. It is a great way to help others.

There are lots of things you can do to improve your communities. Make an effort to be friendly to a new neighbor, classmate, or teammate. Consider volunteering to pick up trash or visiting a nursing home. Donate food or clothes to those in need. Learn more about your own roots or the history of the town or city you call home.

GLOSSARY

arena An enclosed area used for public entertainment.

convention center A big building designed to hold large meetings.

fossil fuel A fuel (like coal, oil, or natural gas) that is formed in the earth from plant or animal remains.

homeless shelter A place where people who have no home can stay.

manufacturing The process of making products or goods.

municipality A self-governing city or town.

opportunity A chance to get something or better oneself.

population The total number of people living in a country or region.

ranch A place for raising livestock like cattle, horses, or sheep.

soup kitchen A place that gives free food to the needy.

tax Money the government collects to pay for services.

transportation Methods for moving people and their goods from one place to another.

For More Information

Books

Kenney, Karen. *Government in Your City or Town* (U.S. Government and Civics). Vero Beach, FL: Rourke Educational Media, 2015.

Kreisman, Rachelle. *Being a Good Citizen: A Kids' Guide to Community Involvement*. Concord, MA: Red Chair Press, 2015.

Marsico, Katie. *What's It Like to Live Here? Suburb*. Ann Arbor, MI: Cherry Lake Publishing, 2014.

McDonald, Caryl. *Rural Life, Urban Life*. New York, NY: Rosen Classroom, 2014.

Reilly, Kathleen M. *Cities: Discover How They Work*. White River Junction, VT: Nomad Press, 2014

Websites

Because of the changing nature of internet links, Rosen Publishing has developed an online list of websites related to the subject of this book. This site is updated regularly. Please use this link to access the list:

http://www.rosenlinks.com/LFO/Types

INDEX